Native Americans

The Inuit

Barbara A. Gray-Kanatiiosh

ABDO Publishing Company

visit us at
www.abdopublishing.com

Published by ABDO Publishing Company, 8000 West 78th Street, Edina, Minnesota 55439. Copyright © 2002 Abdo Consulting Group, Inc. International copyrights reserved in all countries. No part of this book may be reproduced in any form without written permission from the publisher.

Printed in the United States of America, North Mankato, Minnesota.
012002 092011
Illustrations: David Kanietakeron Fadden
Interior Photos: Corbis
Editors: Bob Italia, Tamara L. Britton, Kate A. Furlong, Kristin Van Cleaf
Book Design & Graphics: Neil Klinepier

Library of Congress Cataloging-in-Publication Data

Gray-Kanatiiosh, Barbara A., 1963-
   The Inuit / Barbara A. Gray-Kanatiiosh; illustrated by David Kanietakeron Fadden
      p. cm. -- (Native Americans)
   Includes index.
   ISBN 1-57765-599-0
   1. Inuit--Juvenile literature. [1. Inuit. 2. Eskimos.] I. Fadden, David Kanietakeron, ill.
   II. Title. III. Native Americans (Edina, Minn.)

E99.E7 G718 2002
971. 9004'9712--dc21

                                                            2001022482

About the Author: Barbara A. Gray-Kanatiiosh, JD

Barbara Gray-Kanatiiosh, JD, is an Akwesasne Mohawk. She has a Juris Doctorate from Arizona State University, where she was one of the first recipients of ASU's special certificate in Indian Law. She is currently pursuing a PhD in Justice Studies at ASU and is focusing on Native American issues. Barbara works hard to educate children about Native Americans through her writing and Web site where children may ask questions and receive a written response about the Haudenosaunee culture. The Web site is: www.peace4turtleisland.org

Illustrator: David Kanietakeron Fadden

David Kanietakeron Fadden is a member of the Akwesasne Mohawk Wolf Clan. His work has appeared in publications such as *Akwesasne Notes, Indian Time*, and the *Northeast Indian Quarterly*. Examples of his work have also appeared in various publications of the Six Nations Indian Museum in Onchiota, NY. His work has also appeared in "How The West Was Lost: Always The Enemy," produced by Gannett Production which appeared on the Discovery Channel. David's work has been exhibited in Albany, NY; the Lake Placid Center for the Arts; Centre Strathearn in Montreal, Quebec; North Country Community College in Saranac Lake, NY; Paul Smith's College in Paul Smiths, NY; and at the Unison Arts & Learning Center in New Paltz, NY.

Contents

Where They Lived 4
Society 6
Food 8
Homes 10
Clothing 12
Crafts 14
Family 16
Children 18
Myths 20
War 22
Contact with Europeans 24
Susan Aglukark 26
The Inuit Today 28
Glossary 31
Web Sites 31
Index 32

Where They Lived

The Inuit (EE-neu-eet) lived across a vast area of northern lands. They lived along the coasts of Greenland and Siberia. They also lived in northern Canada and on the coast of Alaska.

Inuit homelands had long, cold winters. Winter was very dark, with only a few hours of sunlight during the day. Anywhere from 40 to 125 inches (100 to 320 cm) of snow fell each year. In some areas, the land stayed frozen all year long.

In other areas, a few inches of soil thawed in late spring. This allowed berries, small shrubs, and other wild plants to grow. So in the spring, many Inuit moved inland to gather these wild plants. They also hunted and fished in lakes and streams.

Days were long during the summer. Because Inuit lands were so far north, they received much sunlight during summer days. The sun set for only a few hours in the late night.

In the fall, the lakes and streams froze. Many animals moved to the coast or **migrated** south. So in the winter, the Inuit moved to their coastal settlements to hunt sea animals.

The Cree were another group of native people living near the Inuit in northern Canada. The Cree called the Inuit *Eskimos*. The word *eskimo* means "raw meat eaters." But Inuit prefer to call themselves *Inuit*, which means "the people."

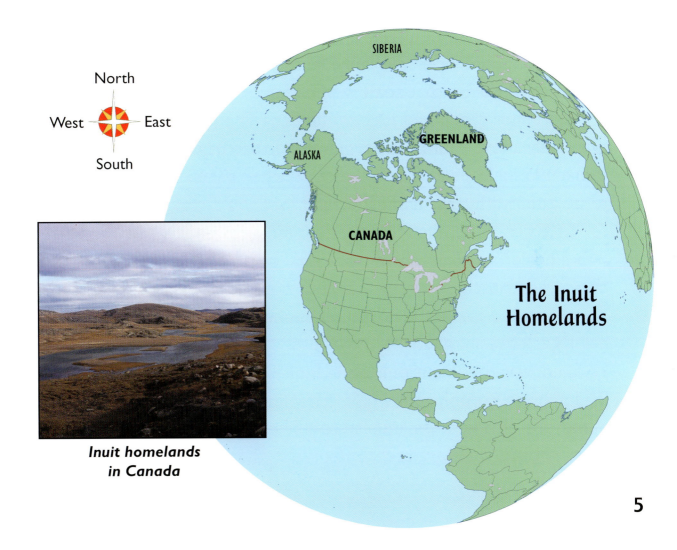

Inuit homelands in Canada

Society

Inuit lived in settlements that contained a few families. A settlement could have anywhere from 40 to 100 people. Laws of expected behavior kept society in order.

Each Inuit group had its own leader. The leader was usually the eldest male. He had to understand the **migration** patterns of the animals and be able to predict weather patterns. He also had to be a skilled hunter and fisherman.

Each group also had an angatkuq (an-gat-koock). He or she was a healer, an adviser, and a spiritual person. The angatkuq performed rituals and songs to keep the people healthy. If hunters could not find game, the angatkuq performed songs and rituals to bring back the animals.

Another important person in Inuit society was the whale crew leader. Each group had a whale crew leader who organized whale hunts. He also kept the special tools needed for hunting whales.

Inuit leaders

Food

    Before going hunting or fishing, the Inuit performed a ceremony. They thanked the animal for sacrificing its life so the people could live. After the animal was killed, it was thanked again, and the meat was shared among the people.

    In the winter, the Inuit hunted seal, walrus, caribou, and whale. These animals were an important food source. The Inuit **harpooned** seals and walruses from small, one-person boats called kayaks (KYE-aks). When the water froze, men hunted on top of the ice. They waited patiently by a seal's air hole. When the seal came up to breathe, they quickly harpooned it.

    Hunting a whale required a group of men. They hunted from a large boat called an **umiak** (OO-mee-ak). They killed the whale with a harpoon. Then the Inuit held a feast.

    In late spring, the Inuit gathered plants such as wild roots, grasses, and berries. The plants were eaten fresh, or dried in the sun for later use. The Inuit also hunted birds with bows and arrows. They collected the birds' eggs for food, too.

In the summer, men fished for salmon, trout, arctic char, and other fish. To do this, they used hooks, handwoven traps, and nets. They also used spears. The spears had long handles made from **driftwood**, and the spearheads were made from antler and bone.

The women preserved the meat and fish the men had hunted. They salted it, froze it, or dried it over a fire. Food was stored in special buildings to keep animals out.

Hunting caribou (above), gathering grass (below, left), spearing fish (below, right)

Homes

In the Inuit language, the word *iglu* (IG-loo) means house. In the winter, the Inuit lived in houses made of snow or **sod**. In the summer, they lived in houses made of animal **hides**.

A snow house could be built by two men in a few hours. First, they cut blocks of packed snow with long, bone knives. They trimmed the blocks to slant inward. Then they stacked the blocks, forming a dome. They packed snow in the cracks between the blocks for insulation.

Snow homes rarely had windows. But sometimes the men cut clear sheets of ice from the river and used them to make windows. Inside, oil lamps kept the houses warm and bright. A long tunnel at each home's entrance prevented the heat from escaping. Each doorway was covered with an animal hide.

The Inuit also built sod homes in the winter. Men built the sod homes about one foot (30 cm) below the ground. They used stones, **driftwood**, or whale bones to build the dome-shaped frames. Then they covered the frames with **sod**. The sod insulated the houses.

In the summer, the Inuit lived in tents. Women sewed together seal or caribou **hides**. The men stretched the hides over the tents' frames. The ends of the hides were held down with large rocks.

A snow house

A sod house

An animal-hide tent

Clothing

Inuit women made clothing from the **hides** of caribou, seal, polar bear, and arctic fox. Women prepared the hides with bone knives and scraping tools. They stretched the hides and let them dry in the sun. Then they sewed the clothes with **sinew** thread, and needles made from bone, antler, or walrus ivory.

In winter, the Inuit wore two sets of clothing. They wore underclothes that included shirts, pants, and socks with the fur facing inward. Over these they wore a set of outer clothes, with the fur facing outward. The outer clothes included a parka, long pants, and boots. In the summer, the Inuit wore only the underclothes, but with the fur turned outward.

An Inuit family in traditional clothing

The Inuit used special materials to make warm clothes. They trimmed their parka hoods with wolverine or wolf fur. Ice does not stick to these kinds of fur. Clothing made from seal intestines was watertight and could be worn as a raincoat.

A woman's parka

The Inuit wore boots and mittens to keep their feet and hands warm. They made boots from the **hides** of caribou or bearded seal. To keep their feet warm, they stuffed grass into their boots. They wore hide mittens with the fur turned inward to keep their hands warm.

A child's boots

To protect their eyes from the snow, the Inuit wore snow goggles. They made the goggles from bone or wood. The goggles had tiny slits in them. The slits allowed the person to see.

Snow goggles

Crafts

   The Inuit were excellent carvers. They carved with **bow drills** and knives made of stone. The Inuit carved materials such as soapstone, wood, antler, and ivory.

   Inuit carvings had many purposes. Sometimes the carvings decorated weapons, clothing, and handles. Other times the Inuit used ivory carvings to record their history. They carved masks to use in ceremonies. The Inuit also carved small figurines of animals, such as caribou and seals. They carried the figurines for good luck.

   The Inuit were also skilled basket makers. They used baleen to make their baskets. Baleen is what hangs down from a whale's upper jaw and helps it filter out food.

   Today, some Inuit men and women continue to make traditional crafts. They sell their carvings to make money. The carvings may show animals, characters from stories, or scenes from Inuit ways of life. They also sell jewelry made from baleen.

An Inuit man uses a bow drill to make a carving.

Family

Family was very important to the Inuit. Survival in harsh climates depended on the entire family working together. A family included a father, a mother, children, and grandparents. They all lived together. Each person in the family had a job.

Inuit men hunted and fished. Men also made tools such as **bow drills**, spears, **harpoons**, and bows and arrows. They carved hooks for fishing. The men built homes and made household goods.

Men also built dogsleds from **driftwood**. Sometimes the sled runners were made from whale bones. Men built frames for the kayaks and **umiaks**, too.

Inuit women prepared food for eating and storage. They cooked over soapstone lamps that burned **blubber** or oil. The women also prepared the animal **hides** to be made into tents, clothing, and boats. They were expert sewers. They sewed hides together so well that the hides remained waterproof.

Inuit men build a sled.

Children

Inuit children were cared for by everyone in the family. The children learned by listening to stories. They learned about the dangers of living in a harsh climate, and to listen to their elders.

Boys learned how to hunt, fish, and trap. Sometimes they caught fish with a line and hook through small holes in the ice. Boys would sometimes go with the men on hunts. This way they learned how to find animals and understand weather patterns.

Girls made small tents and played with dolls. They also had storytelling knives. They used these dull knives to draw animals on the ground. Then they told stories about each drawing.

Children also played cat's cradle. They used string made of seal **sinew**. They used the string to make animal figures. They did this by moving their fingers through the string.

Children also played a game with a small bone pin. It was attached to the tip of a musk ox horn. The children tried to spear the pin through small holes drilled in the horn's tip. This helped the children develop skills needed for hunting and fishing.

Inuit children play cat's cradle.

Myths

During the winter nights, the Inuit gathered in their homes to share the daily events and tell stories. They often told the story of "The Woman from Below the Ocean." Some Inuit call her Sedna.

It is said that a long time ago, Sedna was a human being. During her life, her father mistreated her. He thought she had shamed him. The father **banished** his daughter from the camp.

The father felt bad about mistreating his daughter. He went to find her. She had married. When the husband was out, the father took his daughter. When the husband returned, he saw that his wife was missing. He went looking for her.

The father was scared of the husband's anger. He threw his daughter out of the kayak. She hung on to the kayak with her fingertips. The father was terrified. He took out a knife, and cut his daughter's fingers off. Each finger that fell into the water created a new marine mammal. One finger created a seal, another a walrus, and another a bearded seal. This went on until the ocean was full.

The daughter sank to the bottom of the ocean. As she sank, the spirits of Air and Moon saw what had happened. They gave her the power to live underwater.

Since that day, Sedna is the protector of sea mammals. She controls the number of marine mammals. She releases enough for the Inuit to hunt. She also calms the waters. Sedna is the "Guardian of the Inuit."

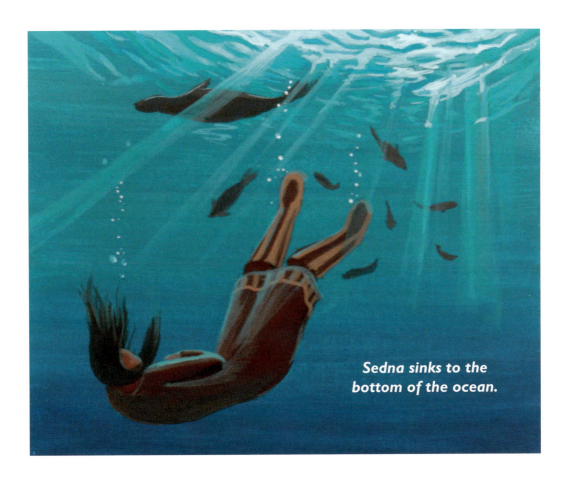

Sedna sinks to the bottom of the ocean.

War

War was rare among the Inuit. The Inuit were a peaceful people. They also lived in remote areas that kept them away from other groups.

Occasionally, an Inuit group traveled into another's hunting and fishing territory. This contact sometimes resulted in a disagreement. Disagreements were often handled at gatherings.

Instead of fighting, the men would sing dueling songs. Two men would face off against each other. They would make up songs. Some made up songs to insult the other man. Others made up funny songs. The man who made up the best song won the contest. The people laughed at the songs and soon forgot about fighting.

Inuit weapons

Contact with Europeans

Sir Martin Frobisher was one of the first European explorers to meet the Inuit. In 1576, he was looking for the Northwest Passage to Asia. In 1585, navigator John Davis arrived among the Inuit. Today, Davis Strait is named after him. After Henry Hudson arrived in 1610, many traders flocked to the Arctic.

Early European explorers traded with the Inuit. They offered metal, knives, tools, and guns in exchange for the Inuit's kayaks, fresh meat, and warm clothing.

Frobisher meets with an Inuit man.

Later, the traders wanted furs. This changed the Inuit diet and way of life. The Inuit began to trap and hunt many animals. They traded furs for steel traps, matches, coffee, sugar, flour, and tea.

Contact with Europeans brought problems to the Inuit. The Europeans brought diseases that killed many Inuit. The traders killed many animals, making many species **endangered**. Russian traders treated the Inuit like slaves. They forced the Inuit to work as trappers.

Whaling ships also came to the Inuit territory. The whaling ships hunted whales. The whales were used for oil and baleen. This overhunting brought many species to near extinction.

Missionaries also came to the Inuit lands. They hoped to convert the Inuit into Christians. The Inuit were not allowed to speak their own language or perform their ceremonies. Many Inuit became Christians. But many remained true to their traditional Inuit teachings.

Admiral Robert E. Peary also spent time among the Inuit. He studied the Inuit's clothing, food, and transportation. Peary learned how to survive in the harsh arctic climate. This helped him to discover the North Pole in 1909.

Susan Aglukark

Susan Aglukark is an Inuit singer and songwriter. She was raised in Arviat. It is a small community in Canada's Northwest Territories.

Aglukark's music mixes beautiful Inuit chants with the sounds of pop music. She sings both in English and her native language, Inuktitut (EE-nook-tee-toot). Aglukark's music joins traditional Inuit **culture** with that of the modern world.

Aglukark's songs have messages that ask for peace to come to all people. Some of her songs tell stories from her culture. They tell of daily life and survival in the far north.

Opposite page: Susan Aglukark performs with Inuit children at the Big Sky Concert in Alberta, Canada.

The Inuit Today

In the 1970s, Inuit living in Canada asked for the return of their traditional lands. The Inuit wanted their lands back so they could preserve their traditional way of life. They also asked for the creation of a new territory in central and eastern Canada.

On April 1, 1999, Canada's government created Nunavut (noo-na-voot). It is a territory run by the Inuit. It is nearly one million square miles (two million sq km). The capital of Nunavut is Iqaluit (ee-qa-loo-eet). About 23,000 Inuit live in Nunavut.

Canadian Governor General Romeo LeBlank looks on as the flag of Nunavut is unveiled at the official ceremony inaugurating Nunavut in April 1999.

28

Nunavut is important to Inuit **culture**. It allows the Inuit living there to have control over their own affairs and create their own form of government.

Today, much of the Inuit diet depends on their ability to hunt and fish. The Inuit live in remote areas, and flying food in is expensive. Today, most of the Inuit live in modern houses, and many travel using automobiles and snowmobiles.

Two Inuit children from Nunavut (above). Inuit women from Barrow, Alaska, sew together seal skins to make a umiak (left).

29

Today, in Fairbanks, Alaska, many Inuit gather for the World Eskimo-Indian Olympics. They are held in July. The gathering consists of traditional songs, dances, and games. Some of the games include tug-o-war, the ear pull, and the blanket toss.

For the blanket toss, people hold on to a blanket and another person climbs on to the stretched blanket. That person is then tossed high into the air. The blanket toss was traditionally used by hunters to spot marine animals on the ice flows.

An Inuit woman from Alaska takes part in the traditional blanket toss (above). Inuit children in their winter furs walk across the frozen Alaskan land (left).

Glossary

banish - to force someone to leave his or her homelands.
blubber - a layer of fat in whales.
bow drill - a drill that has a long movable shaft with a stone point tip, a mouthpiece, and a bow. The drill is held in the mouth, and a bow is moved across the shaft. This turns the shaft so the tip can bore holes.
culture - the customs, arts, and tools of a nation or people at a certain time.
driftwood - wood that drifts on water or is washed ashore by water.
endanger - in danger of becoming extinct.
harpoon - a long spear made from driftwood or whale bone used to kill seals, walruses, and whales.
hide - an animal skin that is often thick and heavy.
migrate - to move from one place to another.
missionary - a person who spreads a church's religion.
sinew - a band of tough fibers that joins a muscle to a bone.
sod - a piece of grass, usually cut into a strip and held together by roots.
umiak - a large boat that was about 20 to 30 feet (6 to 9 m) in length, 8 feet wide (2 m), and 3 feet (1 m) deep. The frame was made from driftwood covered with walrus hides. It was steered with paddles.

Web Sites

The Nunavut Handbook: **http://www.arctictravel.com/**

Inuit Art from Bayat Gallery: **http://www.inuitgallery.com/home.html**

These sites are subject to change. Go to your favorite search engine and type in "Inuit" for more sites.

Index

A

Aglukark, Susan 26
Alaska 4
animals 4, 6, 8, 9, 10, 11, 12, 13, 14, 16, 18, 20, 21, 25

C

Canada 4, 5, 26, 28
ceremonies 6, 8, 14, 25
children 16, 18
climate 4, 6, 10, 11, 12, 13, 16, 18, 25
clothing 12, 13, 14, 16, 24, 25
crafts 14

D

Davis, John 24
dueling songs 22

E

Europeans 24, 25

F

family 6, 16, 18
fishing 4, 6, 8, 9, 16, 18, 22, 29
food 8, 9, 16, 24, 25, 29
Frobisher, Sir Martin 24

G

games 18, 30
government 29
Greenland 4

H

homelands 4, 5, 28
homes 10, 11, 16, 29
Hudson, Henry 24
hunting 4, 6, 8, 9, 16, 18, 22, 25, 30

L

leaders 6

M

music 6, 26, 30
myths 20, 21

N

Northwest Passage 24
Northwest Territories 26
Nunavut 28, 29

P

Peary, Robert E. 25
plants 4, 8

S

Sedna 20, 21
settlements 6
Siberia 4
society 6

T

tools 6, 8, 9, 10, 12, 13, 14, 16, 18, 24
trade 24, 25
transportation 8, 16, 25, 29

W

war 22
weapons 8, 9, 14, 16, 24
World Eskimo-Indian Olympics 30